# CURIOUS KIWI CREATURES

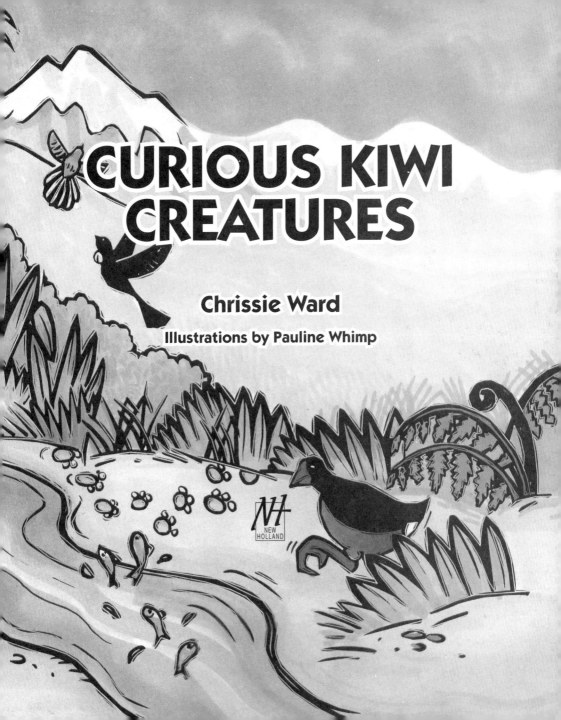

# ACKNOWLEDGEMENTS

My sources for the information in this book were many, including the websites of Auckland Museum, Massey University, Te Papa, Christchurch Museum, Christchurch City Libraries, Wellington Zoo, Te Ara Online Encyclopaedia, NIWA, Landcare Research, the Department of Conservation, and the NZ Herpetological Society. Any errors are mine, not theirs.

I thank Dr Thomas Buckley and Dr Robert Hoare, both of Landcare Research, for checking respectively the pieces on stick insects and the world's thinnest caterpillar, *Houdinia flexilissima*.

Special thanks go to my friend Elmars Polikevics for his help and encouragement throughout the creation of the book.

First published in 2007 by New Holland Publishers (NZ) Ltd
Auckland • Sydney • London • Cape Town

218 Lake Road, Northcote, Auckland, New Zealand
Unit 1, 66 Gibbes Street, Chatswood, NSW 2067, Australia
6–88 Edgware Road, London W2 2EA, United Kingdom
80 McKenzie Street, Cape Town 8001, South Africa

www.newhollandpublishers.co.nz

Copyright © 2007 in text: Chrissie Ward
Copyright © 2007 in illustration: Pauline Whimp
Copyright © 2007 New Holland Publishers (NZ) Ltd

Managing editor: Matt Turner
Design: Pauline Whimp

A catalogue record for this book is available from the National Library of New Zealand

ISBN: 978 1 86966 171 7

Colour reproduction by Image Centre, Auckland
Printed in China at Everbest Printing Co

10 9 8 7 6 5 4 3 2 1

All rights reserved. No part of this publication may be reproduced, stored in a retrieval system, or transmitted in any form or by any means, electronic, mechanical, photocopying, recording or otherwise, without the prior permission of the publishers and copyright holders.

## TRICKY WORDS

On page 69 you will find a glossary containing some of the more unfamiliar words or terms used in this book. Where these words first appear in each entry, they are presented in **bold** text, so that you can easily flick to the glossary to look them up.

# CONTENTS

| | |
|---|---|
| Introduction | 8 |
| This introduced spider is famous…<br>*Avondale spider* | 11 |
| The world's longest non-stop bird migration<br>*Bar-tailed godwit* | 12 |
| Bats that feed on the ground<br>*Bats* | 13 |
| How one bird, 'Old Blue', saved her species<br>*Black robin* | 15 |
| A duck that doesn't quack<br>*Blue duck* | 16 |
| Lotsa legs…<br>*Centipedes and millipedes* | 17 |
| The world's rarest seabird<br>*Chatham Island taiko* | 18 |
| The noisiest insects<br>*Cicadas* | 19 |
| The world's fastest insects<br>*Dragonflies* | 21 |
| Whopper worms<br>*Earthworms* | 22 |
| Super-sized and slimy<br>*Eels* | 23 |
| Birds that prey by day<br>*Falcon and harrier hawk* | 24 |

| | |
|---|---|
| Our favourite fancy flier<br>*Fantail* | 25 |
| Frogs that don't croak<br>*Frogs* | 26 |
| A seal with a warm coat<br>*Fur seal* | 28 |
| Lizards that can't blink<br>*Geckos* | 29 |
| Huge meat-eating snails<br>*Giant snails, Powelliphanta* | 31 |
| Fishing in the dark…<br>*Glow-worms* | 32 |
| The largest eagle ever!<br>*Haast's eagle* | 33 |
| The world's smallest and rarest dolphin<br>*Hector's dolphin* | 34 |
| Precious food is stolen by wasps<br>*Honeydew scale insects* | 35 |
| The world's thinnest caterpillar<br>*Houdinia flexilissima* | 36 |
| A beetle with a 'boring' life<br>*Huhu beetle* | 37 |
| Killed for its feathers<br>*Huia* | 38 |
| A flightless night parrot<br>*Kakapo* | 39 |

Spectacular spiders
*Katipo and Nelson cave spider*     40

A chicken-sized bird with a moa-sized egg
*Kiwi*     41

Endangered wattlebirds
*Kokako and saddleback*     43

Extinct giant birds
*Moa*     45

Ruru, the night hunter
*Morepork*     47

A 'worm' with legs
*Peripatus*     48

New Zealand's first 'pet'
*Polynesian dog – Kuri*     49

A native bird that can legally be shot
*Pukeko*     50

Maxi and mini moths
*Puriri moth and kowhai leaf-miner moth*     52

Bad news for parents!
*Shining cuckoo*     53

Lizards that don't lay eggs
*Skinks*     54

The cat got it!
*Stephens Island wren*     55

Who needs a male?
*Stick insects*     56

A bird with a strange sex life
*Stitchbird*     57

It's extinct – no it's not!
*Takahe*     58

A protected shellfish
*Toheroa*     59

Reptiles as old as the dinosaurs
*Tuatara*     60

A very vocal bird
*Tui*     62

One of our most common native
birds is Australian!
*Waxeyes*     63

The long and the short
*Weevils*     64

Monster insects
*Weta*     65

Not just a good feed
*Whitebait*     66

This bird is bent!
*Wrybill*     67

The world's rarest penguin
*Yellow-eyed penguin*     68

Glossary     69

Index     71

# INTRODUCTION

New Zealand is full of curious creatures – animals that are interesting because of something odd or unusual about them. Some are found nowhere else. Some are the biggest of their kind in the world, while others are the smallest. Many have features that make them different from their relatives in other countries. There are birds that can't fly, frogs that don't croak, and snails that eat meat.

This came about because New Zealand was isolated from other lands for so long. A very long time ago – about 200 million years – it was part of a huge southern continent that scientists call **Gondwana**. The other land masses that were once part of this 'super continent' are Australia, Antarctica, India, Africa and South America.

Over millions of years Gondwana broke up into its different pieces, which slowly moved apart in a process known as continental drift. Gondwana has moved around a lot; at one time part of Australia and all of New Zealand lay within the Antarctic Circle, although it was much warmer than it is now.

For a long time New Zealand was attached to the south-eastern edge of Australia. By about 80 million years ago, the Tasman Sea was forming and New Zealand became a separate land mass. Australia moved northwards, while New Zealand stayed more or less where it is today. Ancient Gondwanan creatures were stranded here: the ancestors of moa, kiwi, tuatara, giant snails and weta.

It was an interesting chance that New Zealand separated from Australia before snakes and marsupials could get here. (Marsupials are animals like kangaroos in which the babies grow in the mother's pouch.) Most importantly, the land wasn't ruled by mammals, as happened in most other countries. (**Mammals** are warm-blooded creatures that give birth to active young and suckle them with milk.) Humans are the dominant mammals today.

Until very recently it was thought that the only native New Zealand land mammals were bats. However, in 2006 the **fossil** of a mammal was discovered in Central Otago in rocks at least 16 million years old. It was the size of a mouse and unlike any other fossil mammal ever seen.

For some unknown reason, this small mammal became **extinct** a very long time ago. So did various other creatures that once lived here, such as turtles and (perhaps fortunately) crocodiles. We also lost our dinosaurs, as other land masses did, about 65 million years ago.

Once the dinosaurs were gone, and as there were no mammals, the land became dominated by birds. There was plenty of room on the ground, so birds evolved to take the place of mammals. Many of them became totally or partly flightless. The most remarkable species was the giant moa, which was taller than any other bird.

Because there were no land mammals to prey on them, **native species** had little need to defend themselves. Some became large and slow moving, and reproduced slowly. Others, like the tuatara and peripatus, didn't evolve at all. Most were very vulnerable when humans arrived.

The first people, the Maori, came here between 1000 and 800 years ago. They sailed from other islands in Polynesia, looking for new places to live. New Zealand must have seemed like a paradise when they landed. It was a bit on the cool side, but it was teeming with creatures.

The Maori brought with them the first animal predator – the Polynesian rat, kiore. The rats found so much to eat that sometimes their numbers reached plague proportions. They began by eating frogs and ground insects, and then moved on to birds' eggs and chicks.

Maori had no domestic animals except dogs, and hunted native creatures for food. The most seriously affected were moa, which were wiped out by over-hunting. Other birds, as well as seals and fish, were reduced in numbers. The places where land creatures lived were destroyed when forests were cleared for settlements and farms.

It seems that Maori learnt from their experience with moa. In later times, when a creature was becoming scarce a **tapu** would be put on a particular area until numbers recovered. Huia and kiwi were probably protected in this way, but the system broke down when Europeans arrived.

Without meaning to do so, Europeans brought disaster. They **introduced** wasps and more animal predators: European rats, dogs, cats, pigs, stoats, ferrets and weasels. Rabbits and deer, brought in to provide food, destroyed forests and grassland. People cleared forests on a large scale for farms and towns. Several native species became extinct (58 bird species alone), and many more were in danger.

Luckily, during the twentieth century people began to realise how special New Zealand's native creatures are. It was too late for many, but just in time for others. There have been some great successes, e.g. with kakapo and the black robin. New Zealand scientists are now world leaders in saving species from extinction. Creatures at risk are moved to islands or to mainland **sanctuaries** that are kept free of **predators**. Kiwi have been protected by law since 1896, but all native species are now protected.

This book celebrates some of New Zealand's amazing creatures. It was hard to choose which ones to include. Every creature, large or tiny, has an interesting feature if you study it.

The book contains a mix of creatures: birds, insects, worms, reptiles, spiders and fish. Some extinct birds were included because they illustrate the different ways in which extinction can happen. The Polynesian dog, kuri, was included because it isn't often written about. Although kuri are no longer a separate breed, their genes may survive in mongrel dogs today!

Some people might wonder why I included a couple of Australian species that have made their home here: the Avondale spider and the waxeye. I chose them for their interesting stories, but they come from Gondwana and therefore have more right to be in New Zealand than, say, the hedgehog does.

In the end, my selection came down to creatures that I find particularly 'curious'. I hope readers will enjoy learning about them as much as I have.

Chrissie Ward
Nelson

# This Introduced Spider Is Famous...

## Avondale Spider

Avondale spiders originally came from Australia, where they are known as huntsman spiders. In New Zealand they are named after the Auckland suburb where they first became established. They are film stars!

During 1989–1990 Steven Spielberg directed the movie *Arachnophobia* (which means 'fear of spiders') about a town being overrun by killer spiders. He decided to use Avondale spiders because they are placid but look scary. The spiders are protected in Australia and can't be exported, but they are not protected here. New Zealand scientists rounded up 374 Avondale spiders and sent them to Hollywood.

Avondale spiders are **nocturnal** (night active) hunters, and spend the day hiding under the loose bark of wattle trees. They don't use a web to catch prey, but wait for a victim to come close enough to capture with their front legs.

Spiders don't have wings, so how do they spread from place to place? One way is called ballooning. Baby spiders spin out pieces of silk like parachutes, and then wait until the wind catches them. They float away like balloons and can travel for many kilometres, even over the ocean.

The most unusual thing about these spiders is their social behaviour. Most spiders live alone except when mating, but Avondale spiders live in large groups of females, males and young.

11

# The World's Longest Non-stop Bird Migration

### Bar-tailed Godwit

Every September the bar-tailed godwits arrive in New Zealand. Their feathers are in tatters and they are very thin and very tired. It's no wonder: they have just flown for a week without stopping, and have covered 11,000 kilometres.

Godwits are wading birds with long legs and long bills turned up at the end. Between 85,000 and 100,000 of them come to this country each year, congregating on estuaries (where rivers meet the sea) around the country. Their Maori name is kuaka.

Mature birds leave in March for their breeding grounds in the Alaskan Arctic. That country is tundra, where the subsoil is always frozen. The godwits have little time to mate and raise their young. There are two months of the year when the sun shines for more than 20 hours a day, long enough for the ground surface to thaw. Swarms of insects hatch, providing plenty of food.

When September comes (that's autumn in the northern hemisphere), the birds launch themselves on the back of storms. In preparation for their long flight from Alaska to New Zealand, godwits go on a feeding binge until half their body weight is fat. At the same time, they somehow reshuffle proteins in their bodies, causing their internal organs to shrink. The stored fat is what they live on during their southward journey. By the time they reach New Zealand it is all used up.

> When the bar-tailed godwits fly north they stop to feed along the way. It's thought that they do this because they can't be certain what the weather will be like in the Arctic. They might arrive to find that everything is covered with snow. They can fly non-stop to New Zealand because they know that there will be lots of food here when they arrive.

# Bats that Feed on the Ground

## Bats

Bats are New Zealand's only surviving **native** land **mammals**. Their Maori name is pekapeka. There are two species, the long-tailed and the short-tailed bat. Oddly, long-tailed bats have short ears, and short-tailed bats have long ears.

The long-tailed bat belongs to a family that is found in Australia and several Pacific islands, and probably came to this country fairly recently. The short-tailed bat is much more rare. It has been here for 70–80 million years, and is so different from other bats that it has been placed in a special family of its own. There aren't very many short-tailed bats and they are found in only a few places scattered around the country.

Native bats have unusually strong limbs, big feet, and double claws on their wings. They live in native forest, and during the day they roost (hang upside down to rest or sleep) in hollow trees or caves. At dusk they wake up and start to feed.

Most bats catch their food — moths and other insects — in the air. However, short-tailed bats can also look for food on the ground. In a very complicated process, the bats fold up their wings, tucking the wing tips into small 'pockets' at the sides of the body. The exposed parts of the wings are tough and leathery, and the folded-up wings are used like legs to scramble around, looking for ground insects. The bats can also crawl along branches to search for fruit and nectar from flowers.

*Many of the native New Zealand birds were losing the use of their wings and becoming flightless. The short-tailed bat may have been evolving in the same way.*

# Two Little Parasites – and One of Them Is Extinct

## Bat Fly and Huia Louse

**A parasite is an animal that lives on,** or inside, another animal, which is called the host animal. The **parasite** uses the host for food or shelter, or both, and usually gives nothing in return. Some parasites have lived so long with their hosts that they cannot live anywhere else.

The bat fly is just such a parasite. It is so ancient that it has no close relatives. It lives on, and with, short-tailed bats, sharing their roosts and eating their droppings. The fly has no wings, but by hitching a ride on the bats it is able to spread to other bat colonies. As many as 10 bat flies may be found in the fur of one bat when it leaves its roost to feed at night.

Bat flies have a level of social behaviour that isn't found in any other fly. Parents and offspring live side by side, and they even groom each other. If the short-tailed bats die out, so will these very interesting little flies.

That's what happened with huia and huia lice. The huia (see page 38) was a very beautiful bird that became **extinct** in the early 1900s. It had its own parasite, a louse that lived in the bird's feathers. Only recently, scientists discovered dead lice in 100-year-old huia skins preserved in museums. The tiny creatures were extinct before anyone even knew they existed.

# How One Bird, 'Old Blue', Saved Her Species

## Black Robin

**All the black robins alive today** are descended from one bird. If it weren't for her, they would be **extinct**. It was a close call – in 1980 they were the rarest birds in the world!

Black robins are native to the Chatham Islands. They are sooty black all over – feathers, legs, feet and bill. They are about the same size as a sparrow, but with longer legs.

By 1900 they were found only on one island. There were no **predators**, but the winds were so strong that the robins found it difficult to feed and breed. Their tiny wings were too weak to fly to a new home.

By 1976 there were only seven robins. Staff from the Wildlife Service (now called the Department of Conservation) moved them to another island where there were more trees and bush. But by 1980 there were only five left; three males and two females. Only one of the females laid fertile eggs. That was Old Blue, named after the blue band on her leg. Her mate was called Old Yellow.

Things were looking bad for black robins. Then a scientist had the brilliant idea of fostering them to other birds. After Old Blue laid her eggs, they were taken away and put in a Chatham Island tit's nest. The tits raised the young, and when the robin found her eggs were gone, she laid some more. This fostering programme was a fantastic success, and today there are about 250 black robins.

*Old Blue is so special that she has appeared on a postage stamp and a dollar coin. She has a memorial plaque at the Chatham Islands airport terminal. She lived for over 13 years and laid more eggs than any other known black robin.*

# A Duck that Doesn't Quack

## Blue Duck

Blue ducks (also called whistling ducks) are found only in New Zealand and are very different from other ducks.

First of all, they don't quack. Male blue ducks make a whistling call, described well by their Maori name, whio. Females make a sound more like a rattle. Most ducks eat plants, but blue ducks feed on the **larvae** and flying stages of insects.

In almost all ducks the male deserts the female and plays no part in raising the young. Blue ducks are different. They stay together in pairs, and the male helps to guard the ducklings for their first 10 weeks. The ducks are strongly territorial and will defend their patch of river against other birds.

Like many other **native** birds, blue ducks are poor fliers. They are relatively small ducks, about two-thirds the size of the **introduced** mallard. The feathers are blue-grey, with chestnut spots on the breast. The bill is light brown and the eyes bright yellow.

A hundred years ago blue ducks were so tame they could almost be caught by hand. Now they are much more shy and nervous. There are several threats to them. Trout compete for food. Stoats attack nesting females and their young. And the ducks are sometimes accidentally killed by kayakers.

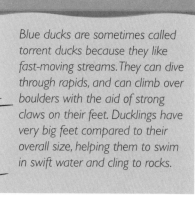

*Blue ducks are sometimes called torrent ducks because they like fast-moving streams. They can dive through rapids, and can climb over boulders with the aid of strong claws on their feet. Ducklings have very big feet compared to their overall size, helping them to swim in swift water and cling to rocks.*

# Lotsa Legs...

## Centipedes and Millipedes

Turn over a stone or a heap of leaves or move a flowerpot, and a little creature with lots of legs might scurry away. It will be a myriapod ('many foot'), either a centipede or a millipede. Despite their names, centipedes don't have a hundred legs and millipedes don't have a thousand, but they do have more than most creatures. For example, there is one **native** millipede with 186 legs.

Centipedes and millipedes look quite similar, but there are important differences between them. They both have bodies made up of many segments, but centipedes have one pair of legs on each segment, while millipedes have two pairs. And that's not all.

Centipedes have a unique feature. On the first segment after the head are large poison-claws, which the animal uses to grasp and paralyse its prey. Centipedes eat soil insects, spiders, worms, slugs, snails, and even small lizards. Millipedes are strictly vegetarian, eating dead wood and plant material.

Myriapods are ancient animals. New Zealand has several hundred native species, all dating back to **Gondwanan** times. There are also a lot of **introduced** species, as they are easily brought in by accident on plants or in soil.

Centipedes and millipedes are mostly 2–5 centimetres long, but the largest native centipede grows up to 20 centimetres. Maori have several names for centipede: hara, hura, wakapihau, peketua and weri. They have only one name for millipede: werimano. Weri means 'horrible', and mano means 'thousand'.

*Centipedes can give a painful bite and should be treated with respect. Millipedes usually defend themselves by rolling into a ball or coiling up and staying still. Some millipedes give off a chemical that has a very strong, unpleasant smell. Robins have been seen to pick up millipedes and comb them through their feathers to keep **parasites** away.*

# The World's Rarest Seabird

## Chatham Island Taiko

Exciting discoveries about New Zealand's creatures are being made all the time. This bird was believed to be **extinct** for 100 years until it was found again, not very long ago.

The Chatham Island taiko belongs to a group of birds called petrels. It spends most of its life at sea, only coming on land to breed. The only place Chatham Island taiko have ever bred is in thick forest on the main Chatham Island. There were once big **colonies** of the birds, and they were an important food for Moriori and Maori. When Europeans introduced **predators** like rats, cats, stoats and ferrets, the birds' numbers dropped drastically.

Chatham Island taiko are very vulnerable because of the way they breed. The male digs out a burrow 2–5 metres long, with a nesting space at the end where the female lays one egg. Both parents feed the chick for about 105 days until it **fledges** (is able to fly). Imagine how easy it is for a rat to go down the burrow, eat the egg or chick and kill the adults.

For over 100 years, everyone thought that the Chatham Island taiko was extinct. Then a bird-watcher called David Crockett became fascinated by the birds. It took five years of looking, but on New Year's Day 1978 he managed at last to catch two petrels. They were not extinct after all.

But they are still critically **endangered**. There are only about 130 birds, and only 14 known breeding pairs. To protect them, the Department of Conservation traps predators in the breeding area. One season they caught 27 cats, 105 possums and 169 rats!

*When the chicks are ready to fly, they climb a tall tree and then launch themselves on the wind. They spend seven or eight years wandering the South Pacific Ocean between the Chatham Islands and South America, before returning to the Chathams to find a mate and breed.*

# The Noisiest Insects

## Cicadas

The *zeet-zeet* song of cicadas is a special sound of summer. It's the male who sings, in order to attract a mate.

He does it by pulling a muscle over a membrane – like popping the lid of a coffee tin in and out – from 22 times to more than 1000 times a second!

The **native** cicadas of New Zealand are not found anywhere else. We know this because they are very clumsy fliers and don't travel very far. There

are more than 40 species; scientists are still studying them and giving them names. Their Maori names are kihikihi or tatarakihi.

Cicadas are found in many different places: coastal dunes, mountain tops, thick forest, open country, and riverbeds. They are usually green, black or brown, and their wingspan ranges from 15 to 75 millimetres.

The cicada has a strange life cycle. Females lay their eggs in a stem or branch. The eggs hatch the following spring and the **nymphs** (the young) drop to the ground. They burrow down into the soil and stay there, feeding on the sap of plant roots, for 4–6 years. This isn't very long in cicada terms; there is one **species** in North America that stays underground for 17 years!

When it is ready, the nymph comes out of the ground and climbs up a tree trunk, a bank or a fence. Its skin splits down the back and the adult insect emerges, leaving a dry brown husk behind. It basks in the morning sun, waiting for its wings to harden so it can make its first flight.

Now the cicadas have only three or four weeks to find a mate, so the males start singing. Each species has a completely different song. The noisiest one is the large 'clapper' cicada, which sings through the night in hot weather. While he is singing, the male 'claps' his wings against whatever he is resting on. Sometimes large numbers of cicadas all sing at once, which makes a tremendous din. They even compete against lawnmowers, as if they think the mower is a giant cicada!

At different stages of their lives, cicadas are eaten by various other creatures. The nymphs can be attacked by beetles in the soil, and the adults are eaten by birds. Sparrows love them!

Like people in other countries, Maori ate cicada nymphs. The best time to collect them is in the night when they come out of their burrows, but before their skins harden. They can be boiled for about a minute and taste like asparagus.

# The World's Fastest Insects

## Dragonflies

The ancestors of dragonflies first appeared about 150 million years ago, and they have hardly changed since. New Zealand has 11 native species. The family that they belong to is very poor at long-distance flying, so we know they were here when this country broke off from **Gondwana** (see page 8).

Although dragonflies don't fly across oceans, they are very efficient over short distances. They are **predators**, catching other insects on the wing. Unusually for insects, they have teeth. Each huge eye has as many as 25,000 lenses, and the eyes are linked by nerves to the flight muscles. Dragonflies can spot even tiny prey and immediately change direction to catch it with their powerful front legs.

Dragonfly **nymphs** (young) live in fresh water and eat insects, tadpoles and small fish. In turn, they are eaten by frogs, birds and trout. After **moulting** (shedding its skin) several times the nymph leaves the water, its skin splits one final time and the adult emerges.

The largest **native** dragonfly is the giant bush dragonfly (Maori name, kapokapowai). Its black-and-yellow body is 86 millimetres long and the wingspan is 130 millimetres. This dragonfly can catch insects as large as cicadas!

Dragonflies are closely related to damselflies, of which there are six species in New Zealand. They look similar, but dragonflies spread their wings when resting, while damselflies fold their wings over their body.

*Dragonflies can cruise at 40 kilometres per hour and reach speeds of 58 kilometres per hour. They can make quick turns up, down, sideways and backwards, and can hover like a helicopter.*

# Whopper Worms

## Earthworms

New Zealand has 175 native **species** of earthworm. They vary in size from the enormous to the tiny. The biggest, which lives on Little Barrier Island, can grow as long as 137 centimetres and is 5 centimetres thick. The smallest species is only about 2 centimetres long.

**Native** earthworms were once common throughout the country, but now they are only found in native forests, old gardens, and in the hills and mountains. They don't like to be disturbed, as sunlight can kill them. They feed on dead and decaying plant matter.

The worms that are found in everyday gardens, in compost heaps and in farmland are all **introduced** European worms. There are 16 species, and they belong to a completely different worm family than the native ones.

The European worms were introduced by accident, when settlers brought plants and shrubs with them. Also, many settlers' ships used soil as ballast – material to make the ships more stable – and the soil, which was full of worms, was dumped once they reached port.

Worms are hermaphrodites (each worm has both male and female sex organs), but they still have to meet up with another worm in order to breed. Some people think that if you cut a worm in half you end up with two worms. This is not true. One half might live, depending on where it's cut, but most likely both halves will die.

*Earthworms are helpful creatures and are a gardener's best friend. As they tunnel through the soil they make holes that let in air, water and fertilisers, so plants grow better. They also bring nutrients back up to the topsoil.*

# Super-sized and Slimy

## Eels

New Zealand has two native eel species, the long-finned and the short-finned. They are very similar, the main difference being the length of the fin that runs down the back.

These eels are huge. Short-finned eels can grow up to 1 metre, and long-finned as long as 2 metres. They live to a great age: up to 60 years for short-finned and up to 100 years for long-finned. Females live longer and grow bigger than males. They eat insects, water snails and worms when young, and then fish, crayfish and even small birds like ducklings.

When it's time to breed, the eels build up reserves of fat and swim out to sea for hundreds of kilometres without eating. We don't know exactly where they breed, but it's probably in deep ocean trenches near Tonga (for long-finned) and Samoa (for short-finned). The young are transparent, flat, and leaf-shaped. They float in the water and slowly drift back to New Zealand on ocean currents. When they reach a river mouth they develop into the typical eel shape, although they are still transparent and are called 'glass' eels.

The young eels travel up river and spend many years growing until they are old enough to head back to the tropics. The adults never return from this journey, as they die after breeding.

*Short-finned eels are found throughout the South Pacific, but long-finned eels are found only in New Zealand. They have always been an important food for Maori. Confusingly, the Maori name for eels is tuna!*

# Birds that Prey by Day

## Falcon and Harrier Hawk

New Zealand is home to three surviving **native** birds of prey, birds that hunt other animals for food. One of them, the morepork (see page 47), is active at night. The two that hunt during the day are the New Zealand falcon or karearea, and the Australasian harrier hawk or kahu.

The harrier hawk is also found in Australia and New Guinea, but the falcon is found only in New Zealand. Although falcons are half the size of harriers, they are much fiercer. They aren't afraid of people, and have been known to swoop down on a farmyard and take a chicken while the farmer is feeding it!

Both harriers and falcons eat the same kinds of live prey: other birds, rabbits and hares, hedgehogs, rats and mice, eggs, frogs, fish, lizards, grasshoppers and crickets. Harriers also like to eat carrion — creatures that are already dead. These birds are often killed on the road while eating hedgehogs, rabbits and possums that have been run over.

The two birds have similar breeding behaviour. It is the larger female bird who sits on the eggs. The male hunts for food and brings it to her while she is sitting. Later, he brings food for her to feed to the chicks.

Not surprisingly, falcons and harriers are often mobbed by other birds, especially tui, plovers and magpies. But the most serious threat to them is from people. Although both birds are protected by law, they are still sometimes shot by farmers.

*European settlement benefited harriers by creating more of the open grassland that they like best, and they are common. Falcons are rare. Being top **predators**, they are particularly vulnerable to poisons and pesticides, which stay in their bodies for years and cause thin-shelled eggs that break in the nest.*

# Our Favourite Fancy Flier

### Fantail

Fantails were voted New Zealand's most popular bird in 2006, and that's not surprising. They are very appealing little birds, with their high-pitched twittering song and their darting flight. The Maori name, piwakawaka, describes this flight. One of the things we like most about them is that they seem very friendly towards people.

Actually, it's not really us that fantails like, it's the insects that we stir up when we walk. Fantails eat moths, flies, spiders, wasps and beetles. They specialise in catching insects on the wing, and are amazingly acrobatic flyers. Their long tail is used like a sail or a brake, and they can change direction very quickly. They also hop around upside down on plants to pick insects from underneath leaves, but seldom feed on the ground.

Fantails are 16 centimetres long, including the tail, with olive-brown back and wings, and white eyebrows. There is also a black fantail, which is found mostly in the South Island. Fantails weigh only 8 grams and don't live very long – the oldest known was three years.

To make up for their short life, fantails have lots of young. They start breeding when they are only a few months old, and can lay up to five clutches of eggs in one season. The nest is beautifully woven out of moss, hair and grass, bound with cobwebs.

To Maori, fantails are special birds because of the part they played in Maui's quest for eternal life. They are thought to be messengers of the spirit world. If a fantail flies into a house, it brings news that something important will soon happen.

# Frogs that Don't Croak

## Frogs

New Zealand's native frogs belong to a very old and primitive group of frogs that has hardly changed in 70 million years. They have many features that make them different from other frogs. They have no external eardrum. Instead of croaking, they make high-pitched chirping sounds. They don't have webbed feet and don't live in

water, although they like to be moist. They have round, not slit, eyes.

Most unusually, **native** frogs don't have a tadpole stage. They develop inside eggs and then hatch out as little froglets. In three of the **species**, the young are carried around on their father's back for their first few weeks.

Once there were seven species of native frog in New Zealand, but three of them became **extinct** when humans brought in **predators**. Before then, the frogs' enemies were birds that hunted by sight, so the frogs' defence was to keep still. But 'freezing' was useless against introduced animals like rats, mice, stoats and weasels that hunt by smell.

The four surviving species are Hochstetter's frog, Archey's frog, Hamilton's frog, and the Maud Island frog. They are **nocturnal** and tiny. Archey's frog is the smallest, growing to 37 millimetres long – that's smaller than a matchbox. Hamilton's frog, found only on Stephens Island in Cook Strait, is the most **endangered** species, with fewer than 300 individuals.

The Maori names for frogs are pepeke, peketua and pepeketua.

---

*There are three introduced species of frog in New Zealand, all from Australia: the golden bell frog, the green frog and the whistling tree frog. They are bigger than the native frogs, croak, and go through a tadpole stage.*

# A Seal with a Warm Coat

## Fur Seal

The fur seal is found around the coasts of New Zealand, with small **colonies** on the south coast of Australia. It has a very thick fur coat, which keeps it warm in the water. The fur is in two layers: an outer layer of stiff hair and an inner layer of soft, downy hair. Both layers are waterproof.

Maori call seals kekeno, or sometimes kuri (dogs) because of their bark. Although Maori ate them, there were still more than a million seals when Europeans heard about them in the 1790s. Seal skins were used to make coats and hats for people, and were very valuable. Enormous numbers of seals were killed, so many that they very nearly became extinct.

Seal hunting is now banned. Nobody knows exactly how many fur seals there are today, but possibly about 60,000. That's the same number that one sealing gang killed on one island in 1804–05.

Male fur seals grow to about 2 metres long and weigh up to 200 kilograms. Females are much smaller, weighing 35–45 kilograms. Seals are surprisingly speedy on land, and in the water they can swim at 50 kilometres per hour. They feed on octopus, squid and fish, sometimes spending days at sea.

The seals come ashore to breed in October or November. Bulls (males) fight each other to decide who will be the dominant or 'boss bull'. A dominant bull has a **harem** of many females, but he has to keep fighting for them.

*During the breeding season the seals are very aggressive – not only to each other but also to people who come too close. It's not good to be bitten by a seal. Their teeth are very large and very dirty. If you want to watch seals safely, don't get any closer than 5 metres. Don't make loud noises or sudden movements. Most important, don't get between the seals and the sea.*

# Lizards that Can't Blink

## Geckos

A gecko's eyes are covered by transparent 'spectacles' that are shed along with the skin. Because its eyelids don't move, a gecko can't blink. It has to clean its eyes with its tongue. This makes it easy to tell geckos from the other **native** lizards, the skinks (see page 54). Skinks can blink, geckos can't.

There are at least 39 **species** of gecko in New Zealand, but many haven't been properly studied. Geckos are slow moving and have a loose, velvety skin. They fall into two groups, 'boring brown' and 'gorgeous green'. The brown or grey ones come out at night and can change colour slightly to match their surroundings. Green geckos are active by day and can't change colour. Both brown and green geckos often have beautiful patterns on their skin. They eat mostly insects, e.g. moths and flies, but also berries, nectar and honeydew.

Geckos can live for up to 42 years and are slow to reproduce. A female gives birth to two babies during summer or early autumn.

Geckos are the only lizards with a voice. The New Zealand geckos make a chirping sound. Another unusual feature of geckos is that they have 'sticky feet'. Their toes are covered with tiny hairs that let them climb sheer surfaces and even walk upside down across ceilings.

Like other lizards, geckos can shed their tails to escape from **predators**. Green geckos don't do this as much as brown ones because they use their tails to help them climb through plants. They can even hang by their tails!

Geckos are found throughout New Zealand, from sea level to mountains, and in forests, grasslands, and rocky places. They are all under threat.

**Introduced** creatures such as stoats, cats, rats, hedgehogs, blackbirds, magpies and kingfishers eat them. People alter or destroy the places where they live.

The Coromandel striped gecko is the world's rarest. It was first recognised in 1997, and only four have been seen by Europeans. There was great excitement in early 2007 when another one was spotted – by a guest at a barbecue!

*What should you do if your cat brings a gecko (or another lizard) inside? If it's injured, put it in a shoebox or an ice-cream carton with airholes in the lid and take it to a Department of Conservation office. If it's healthy, find a dense clump of plants or a pile of rocks and let the lizard go. Shut the cat in the house first!*

# Huge Meat-eating Snails

## Giant Snails, Powelliphanta

Don't worry, these snails don't eat people! They are only called giant because they are so much bigger than the ordinary 'garden brown' snails that were **introduced** from Europe (probably by accident).

New Zealand has about 1500 **native species** of snails. Most of them are pinhead-sized and vegetarian, but there are also several groups of giant **carnivorous** snails. Their favourite food is earthworms, which they suck up like a person eating spaghetti. They are named after Dr AWB Powell, a scientist at Auckland Museum who studied the snails during the 1930s and '40s.

The shells of these giants are beautiful spirals of red, brown, yellow or black. Humans might come across an empty *Powelliphanta* shell, but we would be unlikely to meet a live snail. They dry out very easily. They mostly spend the days hidden away under leaf mould or logs, coming out at night in order to eat and to mate.

Currently there are 21 known **species** of *Powelliphanta* and 51 **subspecies**, but more and more are being discovered. They live in little groups in very different habitats, ranging from rocky mountain outcrops to subtropical coastal forests. Almost every small population is a separate subspecies because they are isolated from each other. The largest, *Powelliphanta superba prouseorum*, measures 90 millimetres across and weighs 90 grams.

*Before people arrived in New Zealand, only birds would have been a threat to* Powelliphanta. *Now they are eaten by possums, pigs, rats, thrushes and hedgehogs. Their habitats are threatened when forests are cleared and wetland is drained. As their habitats get smaller, they find it harder to reproduce. They move so slowly, and can be so isolated, they may never meet another snail!*

# Fishing in the Dark...

## Glow-worms

The caves at Waitomo are world famous. The roofs are studded with thousands of pinpoints of soft, bluish-white light produced by glow-worms. The New Zealand glow-worms are not related to the European variety, which are a kind of beetle. Native glow-worms are the **larvae** of a fungus gnat, a fly rather like a mosquito, called *Arachnocampa luminosa* (luminous means 'giving out light'). The glow is produced when a chemical in the insect's saliva reacts with the air.

Glow-worms are found throughout New Zealand in damp, sheltered places like caves and along stream banks. All three stages of the insect are luminous – **larva**, **pupa** (**chrysalis**) and adult – but the larvae are the brightest and the most interesting.

As soon as a larva hatches it makes a tunnel of mucus and silk which it attaches to the cave roof like a hammock. Next, from that hammock it hangs as many as 70 silken threads. They are the larva's fishing lines. At regular spaces along each thread it puts little sticky, glowing droplets, like beads on a string. Small insects such as midges are attracted to the light and get stuck on the droplets. The larva pulls up the thread and eats the trapped prey.

After about seven months the larva turns into a pupa, which hangs by a silken thread. A couple of months later an adult fly hatches out. The female continues to glow to attract a male. They mate, she lays her eggs, and they both die soon afterwards.

*The Maori name for glow-worms is titiwai. They were held in great respect, for their light was said to be the remains of the original light which existed before the sun, moon and stars. To harm titiwai would bring disaster.*

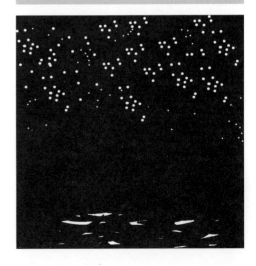

# The Largest Eagle Ever!

## Haast's Eagle

New Zealand's extinct Haast's eagle was the largest eagle, and the largest bird of prey, that has ever lived. A fearsome bird with a wingspan of 3 metres, it had very strong legs and vicious talons (claws) like a tiger's. Female eagles weighed about 13 kilograms, males about 10 kilograms.

Before humans arrived in New Zealand, giant eagles were the only creatures that preyed on moa (see page 45). They were so strong that one would have been able to kill a moa weighing 200 kilograms!

For its body size, the eagle's wings were short. Scientists think that the bird probably lived in forests and perched in high places to watch for prey. When it spotted something the eagle would hurtle down at a speed of around 80 kilometres an hour, then strike with its long talons. Like other large birds of prey, the eagle probably stayed beside its kill until it had finished eating, which might take several days.

Eagle and moa bones have been found together in swamps, which suggests that the eagles probably attacked moa that had become trapped.

As well as moa, the giant eagles also ate large birds such as ducks and other water birds, weka and pigeons. They probably only killed moa occasionally, as moa and eagles lived together for at least 30,000 years.

Eagles were the top **carnivores** in the early New Zealand food chain, and there were probably never very many of them. Their bones are found throughout the South Island and the southern half of the North Island, but only three complete skeletons are known.

It was all over for the eagles when humans arrived. Maori wanted the moa for themselves and hunted them on a huge scale. They also cleared forests and hunted the other birds that the eagles ate. At some time – probably about when moa were wiped out – the giant eagles became **extinct**.

No European ever saw a giant eagle. They are called Haast's eagles after the European geologist Julius von Haast, who studied their bones and gave them their scientific name, *Harpagornis moorei*.

*Maori made cave drawings of eagles and used their bones for tools. Some traditional stories tell of huge birds called pouakai that occasionally attacked people and dogs.*

# The World's Smallest and Rarest Dolphin

## Hector's Dolphin

Hector's dolphins are New Zealand's only **native** dolphins. Although they live in the sea, they are **mammals**: they need air to breathe and they suckle their young. They are much smaller than other dolphins, growing to 1.4 metres, compared with 4 metres for a bottlenose dolphin.

In 1970 there were 26,000 Hector's dolphins; today there are about 7,000. They are split into four separate **subspecies**, which don't breed with each other. Most live off the coasts of the South Island. The smallest group lives off the northwest coast of the North Island. Called Maui's dolphin, there are only about 100 of them.

All dolphins around our shores are in peril. They get tangled up in fishers' set nets. Because they stay close to shore and feed around river mouths, chemicals washed off the land can poison them. Hector's dolphins are particularly vulnerable because they are very slow breeders. They mature when they are about eight years old – they can live to about 20 – and only have one baby (called a calf) every two or three years.

Hector's dolphins are named after the first New Zealand scientist who studied them, Sir James Hector (1834–1907). He was the curator of the national museum, now Te Papa Tongarewa.

*Dolphins eat fish, crabs and squid, using echolocation to find their prey. They send out a stream of high-pitched clicking noises. When the sound strikes an object it bounces back and the dolphins can tell by listening what the fish is, how far away it is, and how fast it is moving.*

34

# Precious Food Is Stolen by Wasps

## Honeydew Scale Insects

**H**oneydew is an important food for many **native** creatures through the winter when there isn't much else to eat. It is produced in a curious way, by small, plant-sucking scale insects. There are 10 native **species** and they live on a wide variety of coastal and forest trees, shrubs and vines.

Scale insects start life as 'crawlers' with long, thin mouthparts like needles. A crawler settles on a crack in a branch, sticks its mouthpart into the plant and sucks the sap. After it has digested the sap, what is left over drips out of its hind end from a short white tube. This sugary waste makes a little silver drop like dew, and is called honeydew.

The honeydew is eaten by birds, including natives such as tui, bellbirds and kaka, and by lizards, bats, and insects such as beetles and ants.

**Introduced** honeybees collect honeydew, but they only take small amounts. Their dark 'honeydew' honey sells for a high price. But when European wasps were introduced to this country by accident, it was a disaster. The wasps clearly love New Zealand: there are no **predators**, winters are mild, and there is plenty of food available. Honeydew is a favourite. It's thought that the wasps eat 90 per cent of what the scale insects produce, so there is less to go round for native creatures.

*When there are a lot of scale insects on one plant, a fungus grows on the honeydew that drips down the trunk. This fungus, called sooty mould, makes the plants look as if they are dressed in black velvet. The mould itself provides food for several small insects.*

# The World's Thinnest Caterpillar

*Houdinia flexilissima*

A scientist who was studying wetlands in the North Island discovered this skinny creature in 2003. She noticed raised patterns on the stems of a native rush, and found that the patterns were made by pinkish-orange caterpillars that were burrowing inside the stems. The caterpillars are up to 28.5 millimetres long, but less than 1 millimetre wide – that's as thin as a cotton thread. In the spring the caterpillar chews a hole in the outside wall of the stem, then plugs the hole with its head when it turns into a **pupa** (**chrysalis**). It hatches as a tiny moth and breaks out from the hole.

Because it has only recently been discovered, scientists are still finding out about this creature. It has so many unusual features that they have named it as a completely new **species**, but they are already worried about its survival.

*Houdinia* only lives in one particular type of native rush, and that plant is **threatened**. The rush, *Sporadanthus ferrugineus*, grows in thick clumps up to 3 metres high. Before Europeans arrived it was quite common in boggy parts of the North Island. Once people started burning vegetation and draining wetlands to make farmland, the rush was in trouble. Now it is found only in three isolated places. The rushes and the tiny creatures that live in them are both in danger of dying out.

*Houdinia flexilissima is named after the magician Harry Houdini (1874–1926). He could be handcuffed, chained up and padlocked in a box, and still manage to escape. This little moth makes an equally dramatic 'escape' when it hatches out from the narrow rush stems. It also escaped the notice of scientists for a long time!*

# A Beetle with a 'Boring' Life

## Huhu Beetle

The huhu beetle is New Zealand's largest **native** beetle, measuring up to 40 millimetres long. It belongs to the family of longhorn beetles, so called because of their long, wavy feelers (they don't actually have horns). Its body is brown, with lighter brown markings on its wing cases.

You are more likely to see the beetle's **grubs** than to see the adult. Huhu grubs are fat and cream coloured, and live in rotting wood. They bore their way through it, munching the wood as they go. They can damage fence posts and pine trees. Many birds eat huhu grubs, and Maori thought they were yummy.

After two or three years, the grubs turn into beetles. The beetles live for just two weeks, and don't eat. They mate, lay eggs and then die. The female beetles lay their cigar-shaped eggs in lots of 10 to 50, cementing them together under bark. The grubs hatch out three weeks later, and start munching …

Huhu beetles have a loud, whirring flight. They are attracted to light, and often fly into rooms in the evening if the lights are on and the window is open. If you want to pick them up, do so carefully. They can give a painful nip if you handle them roughly.

# Killed for its Feathers

## Huia

**H**uia **were last seen alive** in 1907. Today they only exist, stuffed, in museums.

The huia was a member of New Zealand's unique wattlebird family; the others are the kokako and the saddleback (see page 43). Huia were very handsome birds. They had an ivory-coloured beak, bright orange wattles and shiny black feathers, with white bands at the tips of the tail feathers. These tail feathers were prized by Maori, and were worn to show mourning or high social status. The feathers were so valuable that they were kept in beautifully carved wooden boxes called waka huia.

Huia were once common throughout New Zealand, but by the time Europeans arrived they were only found in part of the North Island. Maori had protected the precious birds. When their numbers were dropping, elders would place a tapu on a forest area to stop the birds being hunted there. This traditional system broke down when Maori adopted European ways of living. Huge areas of forest were cleared to make farms and towns, **introduced predators** killed the birds, and museums wanted stuffed birds to put on display. The huia didn't have a chance.

The huia's most remarkable feature was that the sexes had differently shaped beaks. The male's beak was short and very strong, while the female's was long and thin – like curved tweezers. It's thought that male and female birds co-operated to get their favourite food, huhu grubs. The male would chip into soft wood, while the female would pull the grubs out of cracks in harder wood.

*Huia were not good at flying. Instead they hopped through the trees in great leaps, and also bounded along the ground. Males and females were usually seen in pairs, with the male leading the way.*

# A Flightless Night Parrot

## Kakapo

New Zealand's native kakapo – the Maori name means 'night parrot' – is one of the most **endangered** bird **species** in the world. At the time of writing, there are only 87 of them.

The kakapo is the world's biggest parrot. It weighs up to 4 kilograms and measures about 60 centimetres long.

It is the world's only **nocturnal** parrot, and the only flightless one. Its small wings are used only for balancing when climbing, or for gliding from low branches. To compensate, it has very strong legs and long claws, which allow it to climb trees – just right for living in a forested country like New Zealand.

And what's more, the kakapo's soft feathers, in moss green with black speckles, are ideal for **camouflaging** it in the forest. So how did this bird get to be so rare? For a start, its strong, sweet smell gave it away. The kakapo's **predators** – rats, dogs, feral cats, stoats, ferrets and humans – simply followed their nose. The kakapo also had to compete with **introduced** possums, which eat the same food: seeds, fruit, leaves, buds, flowers and cones.

Like all parrots, kakapo live for a long time, possibly more than 60 years. They are slow to mature, and their breeding is related to the fruiting of favourite trees, particularly the rimu, which only happens every two to four years.

The kakapo's flightlessness, and its slow and erratic breeding, made it very vulnerable. In 1995 there were only 50 birds left. To save them from extinction, the Department of Conservation set up a Kakapo Recovery Programme. The birds are not yet out of danger, but DOC's hard work is having results.

*In the early days of European settlement, kakapo were common enough to be kept as pets. Their soft green feathers, inquisitive behaviour and wide range of cries made them very attractive.*

# Spectacular Spiders

## Katipo and Nelson Cave Spider

The katipo is the only native spider that is dangerous for humans. Its Maori name means 'night-stinger'. Luckily for us, it is quite rare. Katipo live among grasses and driftwood on sandy beaches. They make webs at the base of beach grasses, and eat insects such as beetles. It's only the female katipo that bites, and she will only do it to defend herself or her eggs. The bites are painful, but not fatal.

The Nelson cave spider is the only New Zealand spider that is legally protected. It is very rare and is found only in a few caves in the Nelson and Buller regions. It has very long legs, up to 15 centimetres.

Cave spiders are known to eat cave weta. The spider stalks the weta, then drops down on a long silk thread like a bungy cord. It lands on top of the weta, grabs it, and climbs back up to the ceiling to eat its meal.

> There are at least 2,500 species of spider in New Zealand, and scientists are still finding out about many of them. The spiders we see most often, in the garden or inside the house, are not **native**. To find native spiders we need to go into the bush or to the beach — but be careful what you sit down on!

# A Chicken-sized Bird with a Moa-sized Egg

**Kiwi**

As well as being flightless, New Zealand's national bird has many other unusual features. One is the size of its egg. Compared with the size of the bird, it is enormous. It can weigh as much as 370 grams and be a quarter of the female's body weight.

What's inside the egg is also strange: it is over three-fifths yolk and not quite two-fifths albumen (white). By comparison, domestic chicken eggs are two-fifths yolk. When the kiwi chick hatches, it can't stand for the first three days because its belly is so swollen with yolk that its legs are splayed out sideways. It stays in the burrow living on this yolk until it is 6–10 days old.

The size of its egg has helped the

kiwi in one rather surprising way. For many New Zealand birds, the arrival of **introduced** rats meant devastation, as the rats found and ate their eggs. But the kiwi's egg is too big for a rat to roll away or to break with its teeth.

Scientists think that the kiwi egg is so big because the bird's ancestors were once much larger – the size of moa (see page 45). Like moa, kiwi are examples of flightless birds known as ratites. Moa were the largest New Zealand ratite, and kiwi are the smallest.

Kiwi are **nocturnal** (active at night), but unlike other nocturnal birds, their eyesight is poor. Instead, they have a wonderful sense of smell. Their bills are long and slender with nostrils at the tip. All other birds have nostrils near the back of the upper bill. Kiwi feed by pushing the bill deep into the ground and probing for little creatures. Earthworms are their favourite food, but they also eat woodlice (slaters), centipedes and millipedes, slugs and snails, spiders, caterpillars, crickets and beetle **larvae**. Occasionally they will eat berries, seeds and leaves.

Since 1995 scientists have been studying the kiwi's **DNA**. They now think there are five **species**: the little spotted, the great spotted, the brown kiwi, the tokoeka and the rowi. Rowi weren't recognised as a separate species until 2003, and they are **endangered**. There are only about 250 birds, all living at Okarito on the west coast of the South Island.

In some ways, kiwi are more like **mammals** than like birds. Their bones are filled with marrow (like human bones), while most birds have hollow bones to make them lighter. Kiwi also have a body temperature more like that of a mammal – two degrees below the average for birds.

Another unusual feature of the kiwi is its feathers. They are very soft and fluffy, almost like hair. Early Maori prized the feathers for making cloaks, kahu kiwi. By the time Europeans reached New Zealand, full-length kahu kiwi were rare, and were worn only by chiefs.

Kiwi are slow to reproduce. They don't become sexually mature until two or three years old, then they stay with the same mate for several years. The pair has a territory, which the male defends fiercely. If another male intrudes he will rush at it and attack, stabbing with his beak and raking with his claws.

Within the territory the kiwi pair make little shelters and dig burrows where they rest during the day. They choose one burrow as a nest site, where the female lays her monster egg. In some kiwi species it is the male who **incubates** (sits on) the egg; in some the female; in others the pair take turns at the task. It takes 80 days for the chick to hatch – that's two and a half months spent sitting on the egg!

# Endangered Wattlebirds

**Kokako and Saddleback**

These birds belong to an ancient family, the wattlebirds, that is found only in New Zealand. Wattles are loose, brightly coloured flaps of skin that hang on either side of the throat. There are three members of this family: the kokako, the saddleback and the huia (see page 38). The huia is **extinct**, and the other two are **endangered**. Wattlebirds are poor fliers. They hop through the branches or glide between trees, and spend a lot of time feeding on the ground. The saddleback (Maori name tieke) is a striking-looking bird. It has a large chestnut-coloured 'saddle' on its back, chestnut on the tip of its tail, a black bill, black legs, and orange wattles. It stands about

25 centimetres high. There are two **subspecies**: North Island and South Island saddlebacks.

The kokako is one of the largest forest birds, standing 38 centimetres high. It is a dark bluish grey in colour. It also has North Island and South Island subspecies, but there is a major difference between them. North Island kokako have blue wattles, while the South Island birds have orange wattles. Interestingly, the young of the North Island subspecies start life with pink wattles – they change to blue during the first year.

All wattlebirds are now found only on offshore islands or in protected sanctuaries. The South Island kokako has not been seen for 30 years. It is probably extinct, although some people are still trying to find it.

*The saddleback and the kokako are beautiful singers. Kokako in particular have a song that is long and very loud, like organ music. The song differs from place to place, with each population having its own unique sound.*

# Extinct Giant Birds

## Moa

**M**oa were some of the biggest birds that ever lived. They were found nowhere except New Zealand, and they have been **extinct** for several hundred years.

Moa were flightless, and instead of a pair of proper wings they used their long, powerful legs to get around. Flightless running birds like the moa are known as ratites. The kiwi (see page 41) is another ratite. The other surviving ratites are the emu (found in Australia), cassowary (Australia and New Guinea), ostrich (Africa) and rhea (South America). Moa were the tallest of the ratites, and the tallest birds that ever walked the earth.

There were about 11 moa **species**, grouped into two families, and they lived throughout New Zealand. The different species varied greatly in size. The smallest were about the size of a turkey. The biggest stood 2 metres high at the back and weighed about 250 kilograms. The very large moa species are called *Dinornis*. That means 'terrible bird', just as dinosaur means 'terrible lizard'.

'Terrible' is a very unfair thing to call moa, which were totally harmless. They lived in forests and ate twigs, leaves, fruit and seeds. The largest moa could probably stretch up to 3 metres to reach juicy leaves at the top of a tree. Museums often display moa skeletons like this to make the birds look impressive, but they didn't walk round with their heads in the air.

45

Moa were built for running, not flying. They had very strong legs, with leg bones like those of a horse, and big feet. They had a small head and a powerful, sharp-edged beak. They may possibly have made loud, booming calls, and could have lived for 50 years. Females laid one egg per clutch.

Because the different moa **species** varied in overall size, and in the length of their necks, the shape of their beaks, and so on, they all had different diets. This meant that several species could live together in an area without competing for the same kind of food. Three species of bush moa preferred to live in tall, wet bush, while others liked drier forest or scrubland.

Moa swallowed small stones to help grind up their tough vegetable food. Groups of round, polished stones, quite different from others nearby, are often found with moa bones. These are called gizzard stones (the gizzard is the muscular part of a bird's stomach). Domestic chickens digest food in the same way, but of course their gizzard stones are much smaller.

Before humans arrived, moa had one main predator, the giant Haast's eagle (see page 33). Scientists think that moa were slowly dying out naturally, but once Maori came to New Zealand the birds were doomed. Moa didn't expect to be attacked on the ground, and men could simply walk up and club them.

The giant moa became extinct in about the year 1500 and Maori were mostly dealing with the smaller birds, but even those made a good feed.

As well as eating their meat, Maori used the bones of moa for tools and ornaments, the feathers and skins for clothes, and the eggs as water bottles. In some places moa were herded with dogs towards butchering sites. The birds were so plentiful that a lot of meat was wasted. Ovens have been discovered with whole joints of uneaten moa meat in them.

That level of hunting couldn't go on for long. Within a couple of hundred years of humans coming to New Zealand, moa were wiped out.

When Europeans arrived, there were still so many moa bones lying around that they were crushed for fertiliser.

Moa became extinct so recently that it is possible there are some ancient forest trees still standing that sheltered the birds, or were grazed by them.

---

Moa were covered all over with shaggy, reddish-brown feathers — even their legs, which in most birds are bare. Uniquely, they had no wings at all. Other flightless birds (for example the kiwi) have stubby wings, although they don't use them.

# Ruru, the Night Hunter

## Morepork

Many New Zealanders will never have seen a morepork (Maori name ruru), but most will have heard it calling at night. The morepork is a small owl, standing 29 centimetres high. Like most owls, it has large, forward-facing eyes, a neck that can rotate 270 degrees, and soft feathers on the edges of its wings that allow it to fly silently.

During the day moreporks rest in thick vegetation, but at dusk they begin hunting. They catch insects, small birds and bats on the wing, and spiders, lizards, mice and baby rats on the ground. Larger prey is eaten whole, and indigestible bits like bones, fur and feathers are regurgitated (brought back up to the mouth) in a sausage-shaped pellet, which is then spat out.

Moreporks live for 5–11 years, and keep the same mate. Instead of making a nest, the female lays her two or three eggs in a tree hollow, a thick cluster of shrubbery or a burrow. The chicks are fed on small birds, which the parents tear into pieces for them.

Morepork numbers have increased over the last 500 years. At one time they lived only in **native** bush. Now they can be found in pine plantations, on farmland, and even in urban parks and golf courses.

The other native owl, the laughing owl (whekau), wasn't so adaptable. Only a few were seen in the 19th century, and the last recorded specimen was a dead one found in 1914.

*Europeans heard the bird's distinctive call as 'morepork', while Maori heard it as 'ruru'. It is really more like 'quor-co'. The bird can also make mewing calls and screeches.*

# A 'Worm' with Legs

## Peripatus

This strange creature is very ancient. Its ancestors lived on **Gondwana** (see page 8) 550 million years ago, and it has hardly changed since. Like the tuatara, it is so unusual that scientists put it in a group of its own.

The Maori name for peripatus (pronounced peRIPatus) is **ngaokeoke**. They are sometimes called velvet worms because of their velvety skin, but actually they are halfway between worms and insects. They have feelers, and 13–16 pairs of short, stumpy legs. Like earthworms, they lose water through their skin so have to live in cool, damp places. They are **nocturnal** (active at night).

The earliest **fossils** of these creatures come from areas that were shallow seas, but today all peripatus live on land. They can be found in moss on the forest floor, in and under rotten legs, in leaf litter, and under stones.

Peripatus are found throughout the southern hemisphere. New Zealand has at least nine **native species**, but there are probably more – scientists are still 'sorting them out'. They vary in length from 5 to 120 millimetres. Some of them lay eggs and some give birth to active young.

Peripatus are usually in soft shades of blue, green, grey or brown, but some are more brightly coloured. One South Island species is dark grey with orange specks and a double row of green spots along its back. Although most species are not uncommon, they are never found in large numbers. They are eaten by birds, large insects, rats and mice.

*Peripatus eat soil insects, snails, worms, and even catch creatures larger than themselves. They have a fascinating way of hunting. They stalk their prey, then trap it in a transparent glue-like substance which is squirted from openings either side of the mouth. They bite the prey, injecting it with digestive saliva, then suck out the insides.*

# New Zealand's First 'Pet'

## Polynesian Dog – Kuri

When Maori came to Aotearoa they brought with them the first **introduced mammals**: kiore, the Polynesian rat, and kuri, the Polynesian dog. The rats would have been stowaways on the canoes, but the dogs were brought here deliberately.

All that we know about the kuri is learnt from its skeletons, from some pieces of skin in museums, and from folk tales. It was a small dog – about the size of a collie – with light-coloured hair, a blunt muzzle and a powerful jaw. Apparently, it didn't bark. We can tell what the dogs ate by studying bones with marks of gnawing. Their owners would have tossed the dogs bones to chew, just as we might do today. Early Maori gave their dogs the bones of moa, pilot whales and seals, as well as small birds.

To the Maori, kuri were valuable. They were eaten when other food was scarce, and their skins were highly prized. The most precious cloaks, kahu kuri, had strips of dog skin woven into them. Kuri were also loved as pets, and special dogs were given burials when they died.

When Europeans arrived, kuri bred with introduced dogs and ceased to be a separate breed.

*Maori legend explains the close relationship between humans and dogs. The hero Maui went fishing with his brother-in-law, Irawaru. Maui didn't catch anything, but Irawaru caught lots of fish. Maui was very jealous. When they drew their canoe on to land, Maui played a mean trick. He pulled the canoe on top of Irawaru and trampled on him, chanting magic spells, and Irawaru was turned into a dog.*

# A Native Bird that Can Legally Be Shot

**Pukeko**

**M**any of New Zealand's **native** birds are in danger of extinction, but pukeko are amazingly successful.

There are several reasons for this. Unusually for birds, pukeko are good at running and swimming, as well as flying. They are **omnivorous**, so don't depend on one kind of food. Their co-operative social behaviour makes them very successful at breeding.

The pukeko's scientific name is *Porphyrio porphyrio*. *Porphyrio* means purple, but our local birds have blue feathers. They belong to a **subspecies** that is found in parts of Australia as well as New Zealand.

Pukeko like wet places: marshes, swamps, lakeshores, damp paddocks and roadside ditches. They eat soft swamp and pasture plants, grasses, clover, berries and seeds. They also eat spiders, frogs, worms, fish and eels, and occasionally young birds and birds' eggs. The last two menu items make them unpopular with some people, and so does their habit of raiding vegetable gardens, crops and haystacks.

Pukeko live in extended families where all adults look after the chicks. They have a long breeding season, between March and August, and each female lays between four and nine eggs. Sometimes two or three hens share a nest, so that up to 16 eggs can be found in one place.

*It's because pukeko are so successful that they can legally be shot during the duck-shooting season, but each hunter may take only one pukeko per day. He probably wouldn't want to catch any more. The usual recipe for cooking the bird is as follows: Put the pukeko in a saucepan with a stone and cover it with water. Boil for a week. Throw away the pukeko and eat the stone.*

# Maxi and Mini Moths

## Puriri Moth and Kowhai Leaf-Miner Moth

Although New Zealand has very few **native** butterflies (only 16 **species**), there are many native moths – about 1,200 species. The largest is the puriri moth, also called the ghost moth. It has a wingspan of up to 15 centimetres and is usually bright green.

The caterpillar of this beautiful moth starts life in rotting wood on the forest floor. After about a year it moves into a tree such as the puriri, titoki, manuka or lancewood, or even one of the introduced trees such as the willow, oak and apple. It makes a tunnel as it feeds on the bark and living wood of the tree.

Several years later the caterpillar makes a cocoon, then hatches out as a moth. The moths are very clumsy fliers and easily damage their wings, so it is rare to find a perfect one. Adult moths don't feed. They mate, produce 2000 eggs, and then die.

In contrast to this giant is the kowhai leaf-miner moth. With a wingspan of only 2.5–3.5 millimetres, it is one of the smallest moths in the world. As a caterpillar it spends its life inside one of the little leaflets of the kowhai tree – that's an area of about 10 millimetres by 4 millimetres. The caterpillar makes a track or 'leaf-mine' as it eats its way along. When it emerges it spins a tiny silk cocoon on a leaf or on the ground. The moth that hatches out is so small and beats its wings so fast that it is almost invisible.

*The puriri moth caterpillar disguises the entrance to its feeding tunnel with a 'trapdoor' that it makes out of wood chips and silk. By doing this, it avoids being spotted – and eaten – by birds that feed on caterpillars.*

# Bad News for Parents!

## Shining Cuckoo

This bird spells trouble for grey warblers. Why? Because the warblers will have to spend much of the summer rearing the cuckoo's chick.

Like other cuckoos, shining cuckoos don't build nests or rear their young. They lay an egg in another bird's nest and let it do all the work. Their favourite foster parents are grey warblers (Maori name riroriro).

Shining cuckoos migrate to and from New Zealand. After spending April to August in island groups to the north – the Solomon Islands and the Bismarck Archipelago, they arrive in New Zealand in September and spread out as far as Stewart Island and the Chatham Islands. There are no grey warblers on the Chathams, where the Chatham Island warbler's nest is used instead.

Grey warblers build a pear-shaped, hanging nest with an entrance hole that is too small for the cuckoo to get in. She lays her egg on the ground, picksit up in her beak or her feet, and places it in the nest.

After 12 days the cuckoo hatches. The first thing it does is to push any warbler eggs or young out of the nest. The adult warblers feed the cuckoo chick as if it was their own, even though it is more than three times their size.

Meanwhile the adult shining cuckoos have spent a pleasant summer eating insects, particularly caterpillars. In March, when caterpillars are getting scarce, they migrate north.

Shining cuckoos are named for their gleaming plumage, which is blue-green-gold above and barred below. Their song sounds rather like someone whistling for a dog.

*Maori call shining cuckoos pipiwharauroa. They didn't know where the birds spent the winter, so said they went to the legendary homeland, Hawaiki. The shining cuckoos'- return to Aotearoa was welcomed as a sign of spring.*

# Lizards that Don't Lay Eggs

## Skinks

New Zealand's skinks are highly unusual in world terms, as most skinks lay eggs. The only **native species** that does so is actually called the egg-laying skink! The other 25 species give birth to up to eight babies, which look after themselves straight away.

Skinks are fairly common, unlike the other native reptiles, geckos and tuatara (see pages 29 and 60). Skinks have tight, shiny skin, which they rub off in patches rather than shed all at once. They are alert, with good smell, hearing and sight. They climb and swim well.

Some skinks are **nocturnal** (night active), while others are **diurnal** (active during the day). The smallest, at less than 12 centimetres, is the copper skink.

The largest, the chevron skink, grows up to 30 centimetres. Some climb trees, while others live on rocky shores. Many are **endangered**. The rarest, the Otago and grand skinks, are found in only a very few places in the far south.

Skinks mostly eat small live animals such as moths, flies, grubs, crickets and grasshoppers, caterpillars, spiders, earwigs and slaters. Some of them also eat soft berries, nectar from flowers, and honeydew.

During the 1960s an Australian lizard called the rainbow skink somehow arrived in Auckland. It lays eggs, and although it is small (about 10 centimetres long) it is thriving. It is the only non-native lizard that has become established in New Zealand.

*When threatened, a skink can shed its tail. The lizard runs away while Puss sits staring at the tail, which is still thrashing around. The skink will grow a new tail, but it won't be as long as the original.*

# The Cat Got It!

## Stephens Island Wren

The Stephens Island wrens were wiped out by a cat called Tibbles.

Stephens Island is a small, remote island in the Marlborough Sounds. In the 1890s the government decided to build a lighthouse there. Nobody lived on the island, so the lighthouse keeper, David Lyall, took a cat for company.

Every day Tibbles would catch and bring home several tiny brown birds. Although they had short, rounded wings, they didn't fly. Instead they scampered about in the undergrowth like mice. They were most active at dusk.

These little birds puzzled David Lyall, so he sent some dead ones to Wellington. From there they were sent on to London. The English scientists realised the birds were unique – the only flightless perching birds. By the time they could get word back to Stephens Island, it was too late. Tibbles had killed the last one.

No European except David Lyall saw the birds alive, so they were given the scientific name *Xenicus lyalli* after him. We know from **fossils** that they were once to be found throughout the country.

When humans **introduced** rats, dogs, weasels, stoats and cats, the birds soon disappeared from the mainland. Stephens Island was their last refuge.

> Because they don't fly very well, the other native wrens have suffered from introduced **predators**. The bush wren is extinct – it was last seen in 1972. The rock wren is endangered. Only the rifleman (titipounamu) is still fairly common. At 8 centimetres long, it is our smallest bird.

# Who Needs a Male?

## Stick Insects

Some kinds of stick insect haven't mated for millions of years. So how do they reproduce? In effect, they clone themselves. This process is called parthenogenesis, which means 'virgin birth'. Many stick insects do this occasionally, but at other times they reproduce sexually, by a male and a female mating.

If a female mates with a male before she lays her eggs, some of the young will be male and some will be female. If she doesn't mate, she still lays eggs but all the young will be female. What is unusual about New Zealand stick insects is that there is one group that reproduces only by parthenogenesis. They have no males at all!

Altogether there are about 22 New Zealand **species**. Their Maori name is whe. They are found right through the country, from sea level to high in the mountains. Their body length ranges from 5 to 15 centimetres. They are all very thin, and blend in with the plants they live on. The dull brown ones look like dead twigs, and the green ones look like plant stems. Many people think stick insects change colour according to what plant they are resting on, but it isn't true.

Stick insects eat nothing except leaves. They get eaten by birds, possums and wasps. Their only defence is **camouflage**; they stay very still and hope they aren't noticed. They are totally harmless and won't bite if you pick them up. In fact, they make very good pets.

> Stick insects don't make a noise, so they don't need ears. Some stick insects can fly, but the New Zealand ones don't.

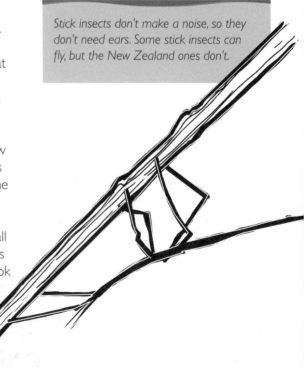

# A Bird with a Strange Sex Life

## Stitchbird

The stitchbird is remarkable for a couple of reasons. Not only is it one of New Zealand's rarest birds, its breeding behaviour is truly unique. As well as the standard pair of one male and one female, stitchbirds can be found in combinations of one male and two females, two males and one female, and more than two of each sex. This probably happens when there is a shortage of suitable nesting sites. Also, they are the only birds that sometimes mate face to face.

Stitchbirds eat nectar, as do bellbirds and tui (see page 62). Scientists once thought that they all belonged to the same family, but now they think stitchbirds are in a family of their own. Their Maori name is hihi.

Male and female stitchbirds look very different. The male is beautiful. It has a black head, white ear tufts, and bright yellow shoulders and breast. The female is dull grey-brown. Both sexes have little whiskers around their beaks.

Maori prized the birds, both for food and for the males' yellow feathers, which were woven into cloaks. By the time of European settlement stitchbirds were found in only a few places in the North Island.

One reason for the stitchbirds' drop in numbers is that their main food is nectar. Now that forests have been cleared, there are fewer plants for them to feed on. They can't compete against the larger and more aggressive tui and bellbirds, which chase them away.

The first European scientist to study the stitchbirds thought that their cry sounded like the word 'stitch' — hence the name. They also have a loud alarm call, and the male has a territorial call like a whistle. He uses this to tell other males, 'This is my patch — get lost!'

# It's Extinct – No It's Not!

## Takahe

Between 1849 and 1898 only four takahe were seen, and by 1930 most people thought the bird was **extinct**. But one man, Dr Graham Orbell, suspected it wasn't. After much searching, on 20 November 1948 he discovered about 250 takahe living in the valleys of the Murchison Mountains, near Lake Te Anau.

Takahe are closely related to pukeko (see page 50). Both bird **species** are strong runners, but takahe can't fly, which makes them easier to catch. Unlike the pukeko, takahe were good to eat.

Takahe have beautiful blue and green feathers, and bright pink beaks and legs. They are about 50 centimetres tall and weigh about 3 kilograms. Males are slightly larger than females. They can live up to 20 years in captivity, but not as long in the wild.

Isolation in the Murchison Mountains saved the takahe, but they were **threatened** by **introduced** red deer, which eat the takahe's favourite tussock grass. Takahe eat the fresh, juicy part at the bottom of each blade, but a new blade grows and the plant isn't damaged. Deer browse whole clumps of grass, and the plant dies if they eat it down too closely. By the 1970s, takahe numbers had dropped to 120.

Deer are now controlled, and some takahe have been moved to offshore islands which are kept free of predators. As a result, there are about 260 of the birds alive today.

*Takahe chicks hatch with fluffy black down and a black beak. They don't get their bright colours until they are bigger. Adult birds are vegetarians, but they feed insects and caterpillars to the chicks to help them grow.*

# A Protected Shellfish

## Toheroa

Toheroa are a native clam. Maori and Europeans found them a delicacy, and at one time there were three factories where toheroa were canned whole or made into soup. Too many of the shellfish were taken, and since 1932 their harvesting has been controlled.

Toheroa live in flat, exposed beaches backed with sand dunes and freshwater lagoons. They burrow deeply in the sand, moving by wriggling their foot, and can burrow faster than human hands can dig.

Their food is plankton – tiny plants and animals that live in the water. The toheroa eat and breathe using two tubes called siphons. One siphon sucks in food and water, which passes across gills that absorb oxygen. The waste is sent back out the second siphon. A well-fed toheroa can grow to be 150 millimetres across and live up to 25 years.

The first laws to protect toheroa closed the season for two months of the year and limited the number a person could take to 50. The rules have got more and more strict. For example, in 1955 the season lasted only two months of the year and the number per person was 20. The last 'open day' for harvesting was in 1993. Today the only legal harvesting of toheroa is the customary Maori take.

*Toheroa are hermaphrodites – the same animal has both female and male sex organs. Each one produces millions of spat (larvae), of which only a few will survive to become adults.*

# Reptiles as Old as the Dinosaurs

## Tuatara

Tuatara are the only survivors of a group of reptiles known as the Rhynchocephalia, meaning 'beak head', which existed in New Zealand 200 million years ago. The others in the group became extinct about 60 million years ago. The Maori name means 'spiny back', because they have a crest down the neck and middle of the back.

The tuatara is sometimes called a 'living dinosaur'. That sounds exciting, but it isn't correct; even though its ancestors lived at the same time as dinosaurs, the two animal groups are not related. The tuatara isn't a lizard either, although it looks quite like one. (Geckos and skinks – see pages 29 and 54 – are lizards.) However, they do have some things in common. Like lizards, tuatara can shed their tail and grow a new one. Also, like many lizards, when tuatara hatch from the egg they have a 'third eye' on the top of their heads. After about six months, it is covered over by a scale.

Tuatara grow slowly, taking 25–30 years to reach their full size of 56 centimetres and 600 grams for males, 45 centimetres and 350 grams for females. They can live for 100 years or more.

Adults live alone in burrows and are most active at night, but they bask at the burrow entrances on sunny days. The burrows are often shared with seabirds such as petrels and shearwaters. The birds' droppings attract insects, which the tuatara eat, but they sometimes eat the birds' eggs and chicks.

Other items on the tuatara menu are worms, snails, frogs, lizards and weta. They also sometimes eat their own babies. This is probably why young tuatara are more active during the day – to avoid adults! However, tuatara could never be serious **predators**. Their bodies work so slowly that they don't eat as often as other reptiles.

Like everything else they do, tuatara reproduce slowly. A female lays eggs only every four years. Mating takes place between January and March, but she doesn't lay her eggs until eight or nine months later. The eggs, which are laid in clutches of 8 to 14, are about 30 millimetres long and have tough, leathery shells. They are buried in a hole and **incubate** under the soil for 12–15 months. The embryo tuatara actually **hibernates** inside the egg during winter. The whole process takes such a long time that a tuatara born today could have been conceived two years ago!

After existing slowly but contentedly for so many years, tuatara were first **threatened** when Maori arrived in New Zealand, bringing with them kiore, the Polynesian rat. The rats gobbled up the tuatara eggs and young. By the time European settlers arrived, tuatara were no longer found on the mainland. Fortunately, their importance was recognised, and in 1895 they were given very strict legal protection. They can't be bought, sold or kept as pets, and are not often given to zoos.

Tuatara are important, but they are not **endangered**. There are about 100,000 of them living on offshore islands and in mainland **sanctuaries**. The islands are constantly watched and kept free of predators such as rats.

Meanwhile, the tuatara go on doing what they have done for millions of years: lie about and snap up insects. As far as they are concerned, humans are a mere, very slow blink of the eyelid. Perhaps they will still be here when we are gone?

*Tuatara take their time about everything. They breathe only once every seven seconds when moving, and once an hour when resting. The human record for holding our breath is about nine minutes. We've a long way to go!*

# A Very Vocal Bird

### Tui

**M**uch of the tui's song is too high for humans to hear. What we can hear is incredibly varied – musical phrases mixed with whistling, mewing, gurgles and coughs. Unusually, both male and female tui sing. With most birds, only the male sings. The female tui's song is actually more varied and tuneful than the male's. She even sings while she is sitting on her eggs!

The tui's favourite food is nectar, the sugary fluid produced by flowers. There are two other **native** birds that eat nectar, the bellbird and the stitchbird (see page 57). Tui and bellbirds belong to the same family, Meliphagidae (which means 'honey eaters'), but stitchbirds are not related.

Nectar eaters have a long tongue that is divided at its tip and frayed along the edges like a brush. While feeding they pollinate native trees and shrubs. Pollen from one flower sticks to the bird's head and is then transferred to the next flower. They also eat fruit, and insects such as stick insects and cicadas.

Outside the breeding season tui travel between forests, rural gardens and towns, looking for nectar and fruit. Some birds have summer and winter territories that are as much as 20 kilometres apart.

Tui are very aggressive and will chase other birds away from where they are feeding or nesting, but they have a strong sense of family. Offspring stay close to their parents and later nest near them.

*Tui are great mimics and can be taught to speak. Maori ate them, but also kept them as pets in cages. Some very clever birds were even taught speeches to welcome guests to a marae.*

# One of Our Most Common Native Birds is Australian!

## Waxeyes

These pretty little birds are distinguished by the ring of white feathers around their eyes. Other names for them are white-eyes or spectacle birds. In Australia, where they come from, they are usually called silvereyes.

Within Australia, the birds migrate between Tasmania and northern Queensland. It must have been on the journey south that some birds got blown off course and ended up in New Zealand. Europeans noticed waxeyes in large numbers in 1856. Their Maori name, tauhou, means 'stranger'. However, because the birds are self-introduced, not brought in by people, they are classed as **native** and so are protected. Like pukeko (see page 50), they don't need protecting; they have become one of our most common birds. This is because they eat so many different types of food – nectar, insects, fruit, fat, cooked meat and bread.

Waxeyes are very sociable birds, and during autumn and winter they move about in quite large flocks. Established pairs stay together in the flocks, but in late winter they leave to set up territories. Pairs remain together for several years and may raise two or three broods each year.

*Waxeyes' varied diet is a good thing for them. If one kind of food runs out, they can turn to another. As far as people are concerned, it is both good and bad. Waxeyes eat lots of insect pests and caterpillars, but they are also very fond of fruit. They can spoil orchard crops by pecking little holes in every apple, peach or plum.*

# The Long and the Short

## Weevils

Weevils are little insects like beetles, but with longer snouts (nose and jaw parts). The weevil family has more **species** than any other living thing on earth – about 50,000!

About 1,500 species are known in New Zealand, and most of them were **introduced**. Among the **native** ones are some record breakers: the longest and the smallest in the world.

The longest is the giraffe weevil, which is up to 80 millimetres long, including its extraordinary snout. The smallest, at less than 1 millimetre long, is a blind weevil that lives among the fine roots of plants like pohutukawa, kanuka and manuka.

Weevils eat only plants, and they usually eat only one kind of plant. When European setters introduced new plants to New Zealand, the European weevils came too. Some of them are serious pests, particularly grain and rice weevils. The female weevil burrows into a grain kernel and lays her egg in it, and then the grain is no good for people to eat.

Weevils also spoil many garden plants, either by eating into the flowers directly or by burrowing around in the roots and weakening the plants until they topple over.

Native weevils, on the other hand, munch away happily on their native host plants and do nobody any harm.

*It's not only large and beautiful native creatures like kakapo that are **threatened** by **introduced predators**. Some native species of weevil are in danger. Early in 2006, Department of Conservation staff moved a group of speargrass weevils from Wellington's south coast to an offshore island. Mice and rats were eating the weevils, and wild goats and pigs were destroying the speargrass plants.*

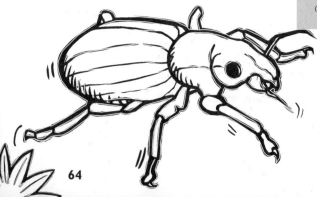

# Monster Insects

## Weta

Weta may look ugly, but they are amazing creatures. They are even more primitive than tuatara (see page 60) and have hardly changed in 190 million years! Weta are harmless to people, although they are quite capable of giving you a painful nip if you handle them roughly.

There are more than 70 **species** of weta, falling broadly into five groups: tree weta, ground weta, cave weta, giant weta and tusked weta. Several species are in danger of becoming **extinct**.

Weta vary in size. Giant weta, which are rare, are up to 10 centimetres long and very heavy. The most common weta, tree weta, have a body length of about 5 centimetres and long feelers. They live in woodpiles, rotten logs, old tree trunks, and under bark. Cave weta have bodies of only 30 millimetres, but extremely long legs and feelers. A stretched-out cave weta, from the tip of its feelers to the end of its hind legs, can be 40 centimetres long!

All weta are **nocturnal** and eat mostly plants, although some species eat meat as well. They are good at jumping and can run very fast. Lizards, tuatara and moreporks eat them, and cave weta are eaten by the Nelson cave spider (see page 40). Maori thought weta were very tasty!

Europeans brought new **predators**. Weta were eaten by rats and stoats, killed by fire when forest was burned to make farmland, and trampled on by farm stock. They are now protected.

*Weta are very tough, as the **naturalist** Walter Buller found out in 1871. He wanted some dead samples for his insect collection, but they had to be undamaged. First he tried to drown a weta by keeping it in water for four days. It survived. So did one that he boiled. Then he shut two up in wooden packing cases. By next morning the weta had chewed their way out of the cases and were gone.*

# Not Just a Good Feed

## Whitebait

**M**ost New Zealanders enjoy eating whitebait, but how many stop to think about what kind of fish they are? Well, they are not just one kind of fish. Whitebait are the young of five **native** freshwater **species**. In descending order of the numbers found in a typical catch, they are inanga, koaro, banded kokopu, giant kokopu, and shortjawed kokopu.

These fish are often called 'native trout', but they are not related to the **introduced** trout. Kokopu are found only in New Zealand, while koaro and inanga are also found in Australia. The giant kokopu are the biggest of the group. They can grow to almost half a metre, although most are 20–30 centimetres. The smallest are inanga, which are usually 8–10 centimetres long.

Like eels, these fish spend part of their life at sea. Much of this process is a mystery. The fish that we know most about is the inanga. In the autumn the adults move downstream to estuaries and wait for spring tides (the extreme tides that occur at new moon and full moon). The spring high tides cast the fish onto the banks, where they deposit their eggs in the grass. When the tide goes out, the adults die, but the eggs stay damp in the grass. They hatch when the next spring tide reaches them, two or four weeks later, and the tiny fish are washed out to sea. Those that survive drift for months, eating and growing.

In the spring season they gather in **shoals** and make their way upstream. The whitebaiters are waiting. Any fish that escape the nets swim on, using a corridor of rivers, streams and drains to reach a place where they can grow to be adults.

*The koaro, the banded kokopu and the shortjawed kokopu are excellent climbers. They can wriggle up damp surfaces like rocks, and even climb up the sides of whitebaiters' buckets!*

# This Bird is Bent!

## Wrybill

Actually it's just the bill that is bent, but that makes the bird unique in the world.

The wrybill is a **native** wading bird belonging to the plover family. Its bill, which is black and about 35 millimetres long, is bent to the right in the middle. Nobody is sure why this has come about. It would be useful if the bird wanted to turn over a stone on its right, in order to find a crab hiding underneath, but no help at all if the stone was on its left!

Its peculiar bill is not the only unusual feature of this bird. It is found on both the North and South Islands, but none of the smaller islands, and **migrates** between North and South each year. Wrybills breed on shingle riverbeds in the eastern South Island, from southern Marlborough to northern Otago. After breeding they gather in flocks and fly to the north of the North Island. There they spend the winter on beaches and mudflats, mainly around Auckland. Maori call them ngutu parore or ngutu pare.

Wrybills don't build a nest. Instead, they lay their two eggs in a scrape in the shingle, sometimes placing a few pebbles around the edge. The parent birds take turns at sitting on the eggs. Both the eggs and the birds blend in perfectly with their surroundings. A person can walk right past a nest without noticing it, as long as the bird keeps still. Wrybills are not afraid of humans.

*If a nesting wrybill does decide to run at you, just stand still for a few moments. The bird will run straight back and sit on its nest. You can imagine it thinking, 'Ha ha! I scared you!'*

# The World's Rarest Penguin

## Yellow-eyed Penguin

Several penguin species can be found around New Zealand coasts, but the **endangered** yellow-eyed penguin is the only one that breeds nowhere else. It is found on the south-east coast of the South Island, Stewart Island, and some of the subantarctic islands.

These penguins are named after their yellow eyes and the bright yellow band of feathers around the head. They are large birds, growing 60–68 centimetres tall and weighing 5–8 kilograms. Their Maori name, hoiho, imitates the sound of the adult's call.

Yellow-eyed penguins have unique nesting behaviour. Other penguins breed in large, noisy groups, but hoiho pairs build their nests where no other penguins can see them. The nests have a back – like a fallen log, a rock, a flax bush or tree trunk – and are sheltered by plants from storms and the sun. They can be as far as 1 kilometre inland.

Unlike other penguins, which spend most of the year at sea, hoiho come ashore every evening at dusk. This makes them easy to count. There are only about 470 breeding pairs on the mainland, and as few as 4000 altogether.

Before humans came to New Zealand, forest grew right down to the sea. Humans have cut down the forest for farms and settlements; sheep and cattle trample hoiho eggs and nests; dogs, cats, stoats and ferrets kill the birds. Luckily, since 1987 **conservationists** have been protecting the yellow-eyed penguins, replanting the coasts where they nest and controlling **predators**.

*Yellow-eyed penguins are experts in the water, diving to 120-metre depths and holding their breath for up to four minutes. Their scientific name* Megadyptes antipodes *means 'large southern diver'.*

# GLOSSARY

**camouflage** – colours or patterns on an animal that help it blend in with its surroundings

**carnivore** – meat-eating animal

**chrysalis** – the pupa of a moth or butterfly

**colony** – a group of one kind of animal in one place

**conservation** – protecting the natural environment and helping endangered species

**diurnal** – active during the day

**DNA** – short for deoxyribonucleic acid, the substance in the cells of plants and animals that controls the way in which they grow and the form that they take.

**endangered** – to be in danger of dying out

**extinct** – none left alive

**fledge** – to grow flight feathers, and so become able to fly

**fossil** – the remains or impression of a plant or animal hardened in rock

**Gondwana** – the huge continent that New Zealand was part of 200 million years ago

**grub** – the short, legless larva of some insects

**habitat** – the natural home of an animal

**harem** – a group of female animals that all mate with one male

**hibernate** – to spend the winter in an inactive state

**incubate** – to keep eggs warm so they will hatch

**introduced** – brought (to a country, for example) by humans

**larva** *(plural: larvae)* – an immature form of many animals that later develops into a different adult form

**mammal** – a warm-blooded creature that gives birth to active young and suckles them with milk

**migration** – a seasonal journey from one place to another

**moult** – the shedding of skin, hair or feathers to allow new growth

**native** – an animal or plant species that has always been found in a particular country

**naturalist** – a person who studies plants and animals

**nocturnal** – active at night

**nymph** – the larva of some insects

**omnivore** – an animal that eats anything: plants and animals

**parasite** – a creature that lives on or inside another animal

**predator** – an animal that hunts, kills and eats other animals

**pupa** – the third stage in the life cycle of many insects, during which it doesn't move or feed

**refuge** – a safe place

**sanctuary** – see refuge

**shoal** – a large group of fish

**species** – a population of plants or animals whose members are so alike that they are able to breed with one another

**subspecies** – a population of plants or animals that forms a portion of a species

**specimen** – an individual that is seen as typical of its species

**tapu** *(Maori)* – to be restricted, forbidden or sacred

**threatened** – in danger of becoming

# INDEX

Avondale spider 11
bar-tailed godwit 12
bat, short-tailed and long-tailed 13–14
bat fly 14
bellbird 35, 57, 62
black robin 15
blue duck 16
Buller, Walter 65
bush wren 55
cave spider, Nelson 40, 65
centipede 17
Chatham Island taiko 18
Chatham Island warbler 53
Chatham Islands 15, 18, 53
cicada 19–20
Crockett, David 71
cuckoo, shining 53
Department of Conservation 15, 18, 30, 39, 64
dog, Polynesian 49
dolphin, Hector's 34
    Maui's 34
dragonflies 21
duck, blue 16
earthworm 22
eagle, Haast's 33, 46
eel 23
falcon 24
fantail 25

frog 26–27
fur seal 28
gecko 29–30, 54
giant snail 31
glow-worm 32
godwit, bar-tailed 12
Gondwana 8, 10, 69
grey warbler 53
Haast's eagle 33, 46
harrier hawk 24
Hector's dolphin 34
honeydew scale insect 35
*Houdinia flexilissima* 36
huhu beetle 37
huia 9, 14, 38, 43
huia louse 14
kaka 35
kakapo 10, 39, 64
katipo 40
kiore (see Polynesian rat) 9, 49, 61
kiwi 8, 9, 10, 41–42, 45
kokako 38, 43, 44
kowhai leaf miner moth 52
kuri (see Polynesian dog) 49
laughing owl 47
lizard 17, 24, 29, 30, 60, 61
long-tailed bat 13–14
louse, huia 14
Lyall, David 55

Maui's dolphin 34
millipede 17, 42
moa 8, 9, 33, 41, 42, 45–46
morepork 24, 47, 65
moth, kowhai leaf miner 52
    puriri 52
Nelson cave spider 40, 65
Orbell, Graham 58
owl
    morepork 24, 47, 65
    laughing 47
penguin, yellow-eyed 68
peripatus 48
plover 24, 67
Polynesian dog 49
Polynesian rat 9, 49, 61
Powelliphanta (see snail, giant) 31
pukeko 50–51, 59, 63
puriri moth 52
rat, Polynesian 9, 49, 61
rifleman 55
robin 10, 15, 17
rock wren 55
saddleback 38, 43–44
scale insect 35
seal, fur 28
shining cuckoo 53
short-tailed bat 13–14
silvereye (see waxeye) 63

skink 29, 54, 60
snail, giant 31
spider, Avondale 11
spider, Nelson cave 40, 65
    Avondale 11
    katipo 40
Stephens Island 27, 55
Stephens Island wren 55
Stewart Island 53, 68
stick insect 56
stitchbird 57, 62
taiko, Chatham Island 18
takahe 58
toheroa 59
trout 16, 21, 66
tuatara 8, 9, 60–61
tui 24, 35, 57
Waitomo Caves 32
warbler, grey 53
    Chatham Island 53
wattlebird 38, 43–44
waxeye 10, 63
weevil 64
weta 8, 40, 61, 65
whitebait 66
wren, Stephens Island 55
    rock 55
wrybill 67
yellow-eyed penguin 68